I Am a Doctor Too

"What Type of Doctor Am I?"

Daphney Maurisseau Carter
MSN, ARNP, FNP-BC

Copyright © 2017   Daphney Maurisseau Carter

All rights reserved. No part of this publication may be reproduced, distributed, or transmitted in any form or by any means, including photocopying, recording, or other electronic or mechanical methods, without the prior written permission of the publisher, except in the case of brief quotations embodied in critical reviews and certain other noncommercial uses permitted by copyright law.

ISBN-13: 978-1945532191
ISBN-10: 194553219X

Published by Opportune Independent Publishing Company
Illustrated by Keira LaRaque

Printed in the United States of America
For permission requests, write to the publisher, addressed "Attention: Permissions Coordinator," at the address below.
info@opportunepublishing.com
www. opportunepublishing.com

ABOUT I CAN BE FOUNDATION INC

I Can Be Foundation Inc. is a 501 (c) 3 nonprofit organization that develops programs and host events that emphasizes the importance of literacy in our youth.

In addition, the I Can Be Foundation Inc.'s events spotlights child entrepreneurs by providing a platform to showcase their businesses and/or foundations.

The I Can Be Foundation Inc. seeks to empower and educate children of all ages via the I Can Be Books series. These books provide our youth with early exposure to both traditional and non-traditional careers.

The I Can Be Foundation Inc. keys to success are to READ. LEARN. BEELIEVE. ACHIEVE. REPEAT.

Hello _____!
(Name)

We are all doctors that provide special care for our patients. We can treat them at our office, but if they're really sick, we may have to take care of him/her at the hospital. Usually all you need is one doctor at a time. However, there are times when we work together as a team to make sure our patients get back to good health. As you read along, you can guess what types of doctors each of us are.

I specialize in treating patients who have disorders of their brain or spinal cord. I am checking Timothy's knee reflexes with a percussion hammer. By doing this, I will know if he has problems with his spinal cord.

WHAT KIND OF DOCTOR AM I?

**Neurologist [noo-rol-uh-jist]
Brain & Spinal Cord Doctor**

If you have a problems going to pee, I am the doctor to see. Daniel is finally going home from the hospital today. But first, I am teaching him how to use a leg bag.

WHAT KIND OF DOCTOR AM I?

Urologist [yoo-rol-uh-jist]

I care for patients with blood disorders. Monique has Sickle Cell Disease. I am teaching her the difference between a healthy red blood cell and a sickled cell.

WHAT KIND OF DOCTOR AM I?

**Hematologist [hee-muh-tol-uh-jist]
Blood Cell Doctor**

I take care of patients with kidney disorders. Mr. Bowman is using a dialysis machine because his kidneys aren't working properly. The machine acts like a real kidney to keep him healthy.

WHAT TYPE OF DOCTOR AM I?

**Nephrologist [nuh-frol-uh-jist]
Kidney Doctor**

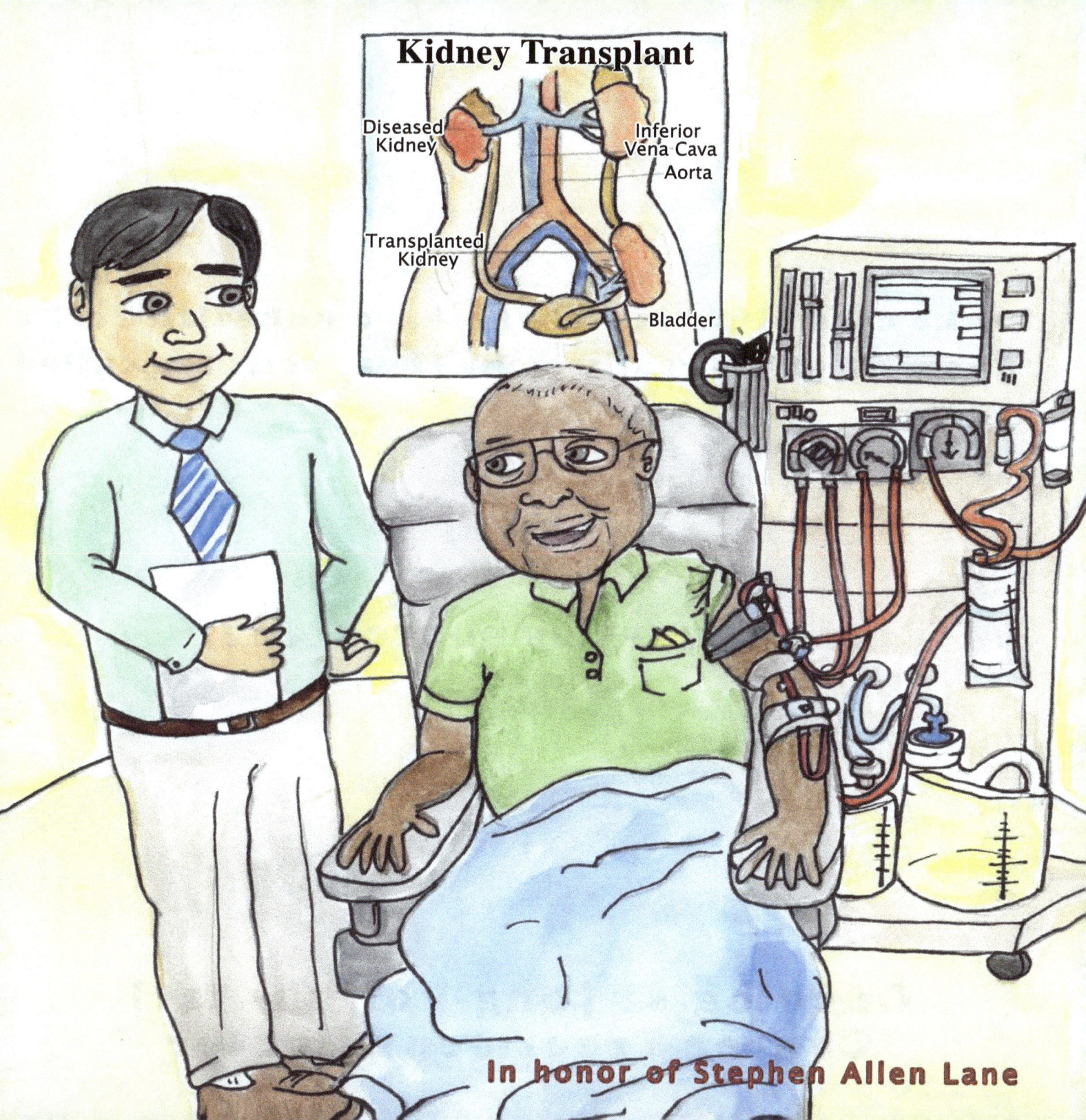

I take care of patients who have unhealthy cells that make them really sick. These cells are called cancer.

WHAT TYPE OF DOCTOR AM I?

**Oncologist [ong-kol-uh-jist]
Cancer Treatment Doctor**

"YES, RAYNA CAN!"
In honor of
Rayna Darden

I diagnose and treat (take care of) lung diseases. Stephanie sometimes has difficulty breathing. I am teaching her the proper way to use an inhaler. The medicine in the inhaler will help her breathe better.

WHAT KIND OF DOCTOR AM I?

**Pulmonologist [poŏl'mə·nol'ə·jist]
Lung Doctor**

I help my patients with exercises to help them get better. Mrs. Evans' back is hurting her. My job is to help get her back muscles stronger and feel better.

WHAT TYPE OF DOCTOR AM I?

**Physical Therapist/Physiatrist
[fiz-ee-a-trist]
Pain Doctor**

I help diagnose and treat diseases of all women. During their yearly check ups, I teach them how to keep their bodies healthy.

WHAT KIND OF DOCTOR AM I?

**Gynecologist [gahy-ni-kol-uh-jist]
Women's Health Doctor**

If your tummy hurts, come to my office. I will look for bulges and listen to your belly sounds with my stethoscope. I will then press on your belly. This is how I can diagnose a problem.

WHAT KIND OF DOCTOR AM I?

**Gastroenterologist
[gas-troh-en-tuh-rol-uh-jist]
Stomach Doctor**

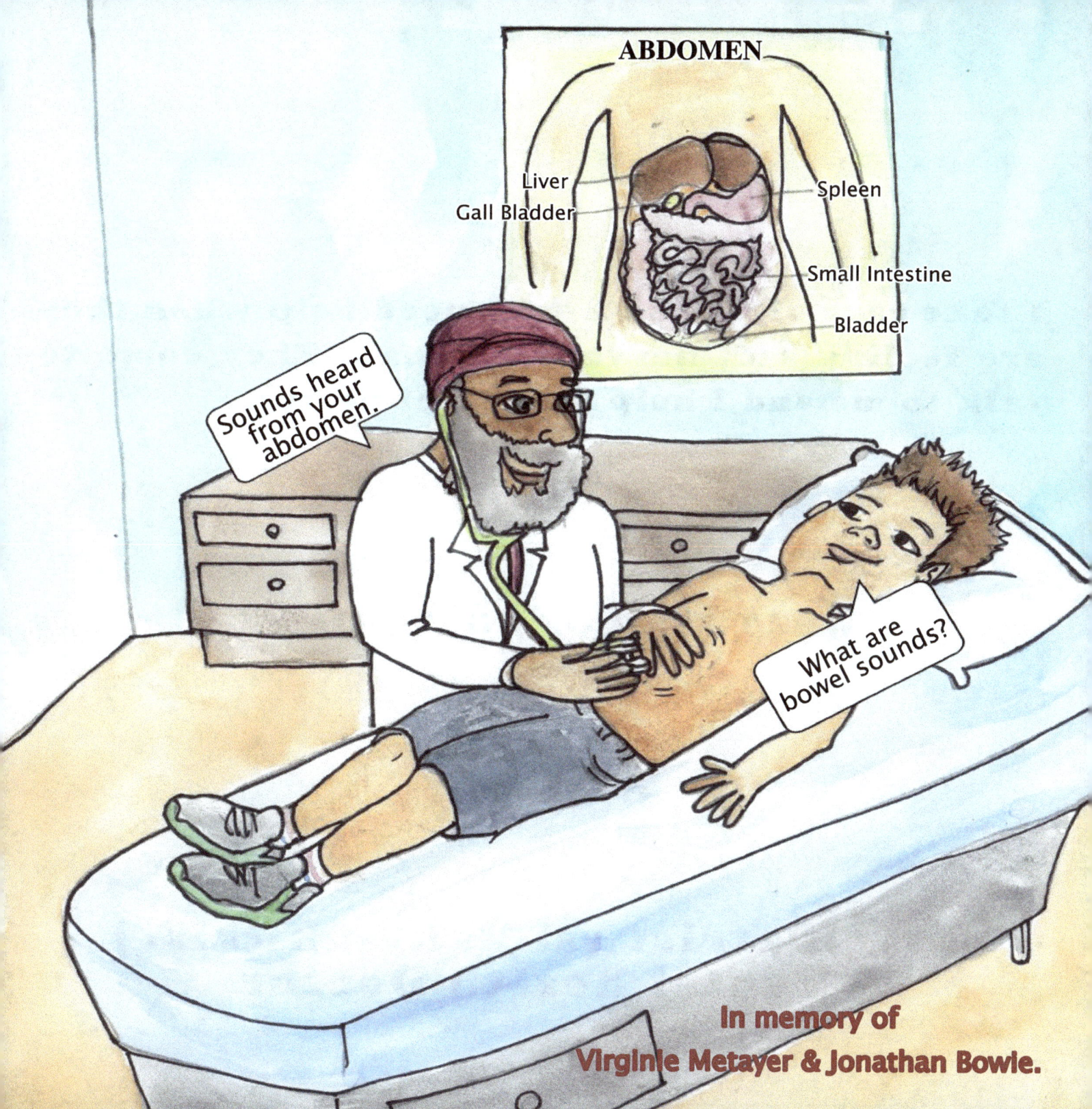

I take care of patients who need help when they are feeling sad, nervous, or mad. They come to talk to me and I help them feel better.

WHAT KIND OF DOCTOR AM I?

**Psychiatrist [si-kahy-uh-trist]
Mental Health Doctor**

If you have broken bones and joints, I am the doctor to see. Sometimes, I have to perform surgery to fix your broken body part.

WHAT KIND OF DOCTOR AM I?

**Orthopedic [awr-thuh-pee-dik]
Pain & Joints Doctor**

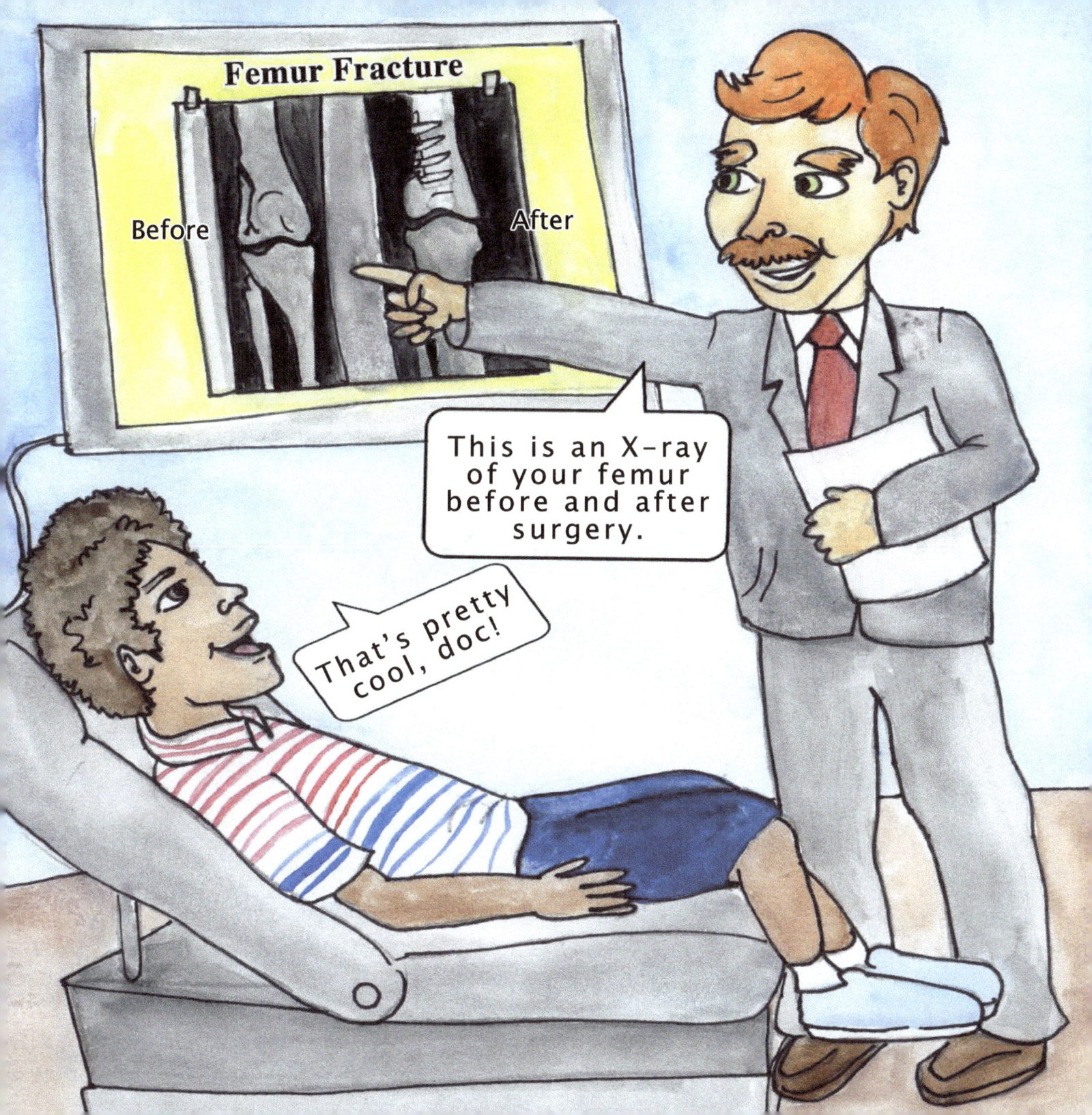

What kind of doctor will you be?

Glossary

Abdomen — Belly
Cancer — Unhealthy or bad cells
Diagnose — Find; look for; identify; spot
Disease/Disorders — Health problems; illnesses; sicknesses
Prevent — To stop
Specialize — To focus; to study
Treat — Take care of; heal; cure
Urinate — Pee

www.ingramcontent.com/pod-product-compliance
Lightning Source LLC
Chambersburg PA
CBHW081358080526
44588CB00016B/2540